GOODNIGHT ZOO

ALEXA ASAGI ANDRES

I0169103

Published by Yawn's Publishing
198 North Street
Canton, GA 30114
www.yawnspublishing.com

Library of Congress Control Number: 2016950168

ISBN13: 978-1-943529-61-2

Printed in the United States

Cover and interior photos by Darla Andres

Dedicated to my amazing mother, Darla Andres, who has always helped inspire me, support me, humor me, and most importantly create with me, she has always been there for me as a writer, a mother, a helper of my GAD/SPD and most importantly my friend

I also dedicate this book to my grandmother, Gloria Davis, who has been my second biggest supporter, a driving force in my life encouraging me to write, to publish and to go wherever my heart takes me

Thank you to you both for being the women you are and for tuning out all of the unstrange people who have criticized you for it, thank you for believing that strangeness- difference- is not wrongness as most people believe

Special thanks to my aunt Suzanne Andres who provided the photo for my biography, my grandfather Harold Davis for his enthusiasm, my closest friend and writing buddy Nicole Long for her support, my dad Tony Andres for giving me my determination (stubbornness), and to my puppy Isabo McKenzie Andres for being one of the strangest creatures I've ever met (and that's saying a lot)

Bonus thanks to my most loyal supporters, Stevie, Jamie, Branda, and Marie- I can always count on you for a conversation, a read, and a smile, thank you for adding so much to my life, hugs and werewolf cuddles to anyone who picks up my books, know that any smile they give you gives me a smile right back!

Extra special thanks to Darla Andres again for the AMAZING photos she captured! As well as Bart Clennon, for his help in getting this book off the ground, Rachel Davis, Jeff Cox, and the people of Zoo Atlanta for allowing us to photograph their animals for this book, I've been a long time super fan of Zoo Atlanta and it's a dream come true to be including them in one of my books, thanks again!

Goodnight, goodnight to the animals in the zoo

The day is gone, there's nothing left to do

Goodnight Flamingos, time to curl up tight

Sleeping on one leg all through the night

Goodnight Elephants, it's long after dusk

Rest your heavy heads, and your even heavier tusks

Goodnight Rhinos, nod off and dream

You look much more peaceful than you usually seem

Goodnight Giraffes, you sleep standing still

You've found such a nice place at the top of the hill

Goodnight Zebras, no two of you look the same

It must take forever to say goodnight by each name

Goodnight Birdies, it's time to sleep

Quiet your songs now, don't make a peep

Goodnight Alligators, stay dry on land

No need to fall asleep in the water
and need a helping hand

Goodnight Meerkats, stay above ground

You're such peaceful sleepers, never making a sound

Goodnight Warthogs, time to shut your doors

Don't wake the others with your loud little snores

Goodnight Lions, time to go in

You're looking snug in your cozy den

Goodnight Lemurs, snuggle up in your trees

It's been a long day, time to catch some Zzzs

Goodnight Gorillas, I hope you're staying warm

It looks like rain, I hope there isn't a storm

Goodnight Naked Mole Rats, it's time for you to wake up

You wake during the night, every elder and every pup

Goodnight Fossas, you're nocturnal too

Just another night-dweller living at the zoo

Goodnight Sun Bears, you've had a lazy day

But you'd still rather sleep than go out and play

Goodnight Bush Dogs, it's sleepy time for you

You'll wake tomorrow to the smell of morning dew

Goodnight Tigers, your yawns sound like roars

I wonder if the rest of the zoo will hear your snores

Goodnight Otters, you're all snuggling in a pile

But you might decide to stretch out, every once in a while

Goodnight Lizards, I hope you've had a nice day

Make sure to get some sleep so tomorrow you can play

Goodnight Snakes, some on the ground and some in trees

I hope you're curling up to sleep tonight with ease

Goodnight Orangutans, you're at peace in your trees

It must be nice to sleep whenever you please

Goodnight Tanukis, you're looking happy

I won't mention how cute you are, I don't want to be sappy

Goodnight Kangaroos, lay down and get some rest

Make sure to sleep well so you can be at your best

Goodnight Pandas, are you full and content?

We want you to wake up at one hundred percent

Goodnight Sloths, you're usually kind of slow

But you fall asleep quickly, that much I know

Goodnight Binturongs, you're awake in the day and at night

You take plenty of naps though, so it's quite alright

Goodnight Petting Zoo, time for you to sleep

I don't suppose you need any help counting sheep

Goodnight Tamarins, you're suddenly so still

You're always so active, but now you've had your fill

So goodnight, goodnight, goodnight to the zoo

And goodnight, sleep well, goodnight to you too

Other Books By Alexa

-They Call Me Strange
-Little Jars Of Your Soul
-Monsters Under The Bed
-Faery Tales, Mermaid Myths, And Other Fantastical Legends Vol. 1
-Faery Tales, Mermaid Myths, And Other Fantastical Legends Vol. 2
-Chillers Vol. 1
-Chillers Vol. 2
-Poetry And Ponderings Vol. 1
-Poetry And Ponderings Vol. 2

www.ingramcontent.com/pod-product-compliance
Lightning Source LLC
Chambersburg PA
CBHW041435040426
42452CB00023B/2986